SCHIRMER'S LIBRARY
OF MUSICAL CLASSICS

Vol. 1738

PAUL DUKAS

The Sorcerer's Apprentice

For Piano

Transcribed for Piano by
GYORGY SANDOR

ISBN 0-7935-1745-1

G. SCHIRMER, Inc.

DISTRIBUTED BY

HAL•LEONARD®
CORPORATION
7777 W. BLUEMOUND RD. P.O. BOX 13819 MILWAUKEE, WI 53213

The Sorcerer's Apprentice
Scherzo
(After a Ballade by Goethe)

2

Vif ♩. = 126 (*three measures in one unit, as if* 9/8)

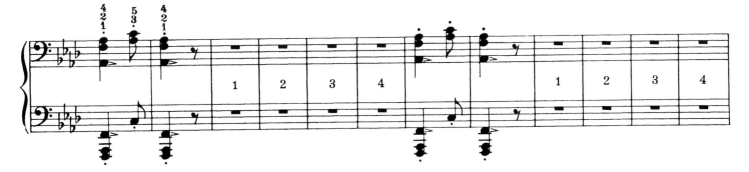

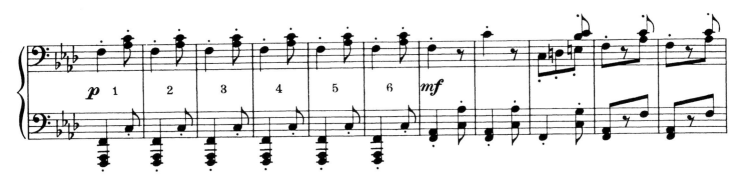

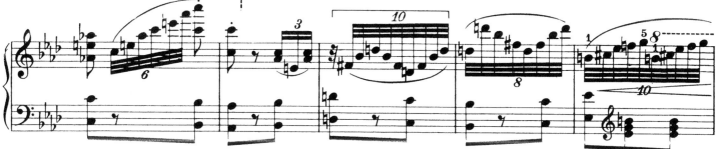

poco stringendo

a tempo　　　　　*scherzando*

subito

quasi pizz.　　　　　*pp*

mf

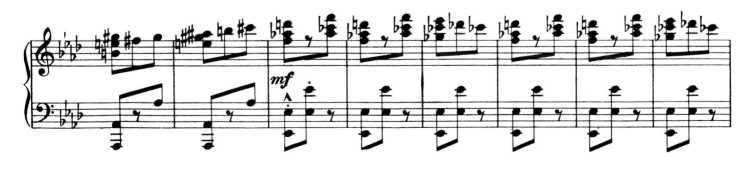

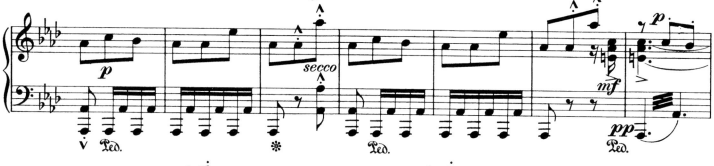

Toujours plus animé

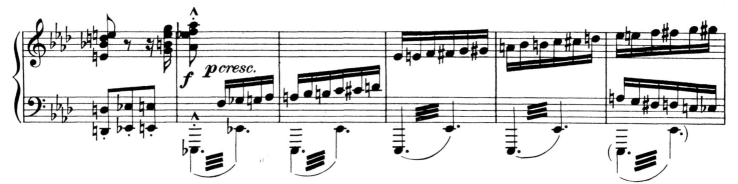

Très vif

Retenu

Plus retenu ♩. = 80

poco a poco accelerando al _ _ _ _ _ _

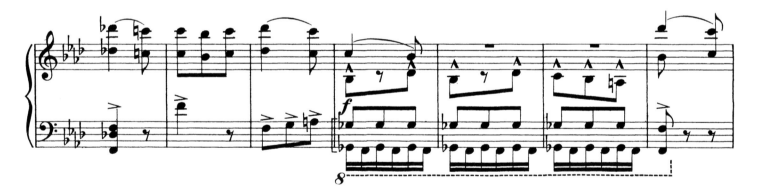

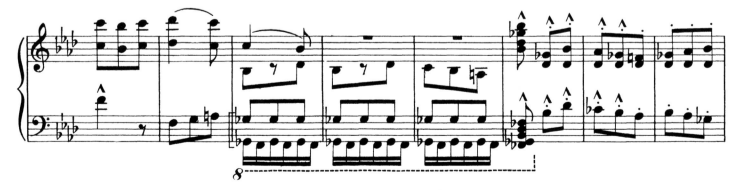

En animant un peu

Toujours plus animé

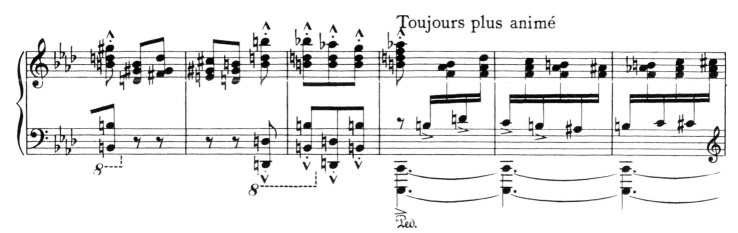

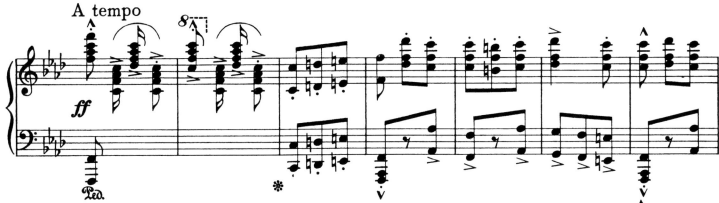

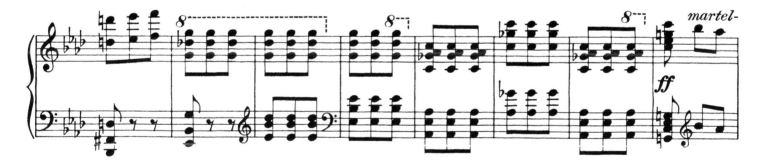

Plus animé

En animant toujours

Assez lent

poco rallentando

Vif